A
CHILD'S FIRST
STEPS TO
VIRTUES

Written and Illustrated by
Emily Hunter

HARVEST HOUSE PUBLISHERS
Eugene, Oregon 97402

Scripture quotations in this book are taken from the King James Version of the Bible.

A CHILD'S FIRST STEPS TO VIRTUES
Formerly titled
A Child's First Book of Virtues

Copyright © 1995 Emily Hunter
Published by Harvest House Publishers
Eugene, Oregon 97402

Library of Congress Cataloging-in-Publication Data
Hunter, Emily, 1919-
[Child's first book of virtues]
A child's first steps to virtues / Emily Hunter.
p. cm.
"Formerly titled A child's first book of virtues"—T.p. verso.
Summary: A collection of over 100 short stories and rhymes that illustrate
the virtues of generosity, honesty, compassion, loyalty, and others.
ISBN 1-56507-626-5
1. Children's literature, American.   2. Virtues—Literary collections
[1. Conduct of life—Literary collections.
2. Christian life—Literary collections.]   I. Title.
PZ7.H91662Cj   1997
[E]—dc21   96-48870
CIP
AC

Certain illustrations in this book are adapted from
illustrations in *The Bible-Time Nursery Rhyme Book*
© 1981 by Emily Hunter, *My Bedtime Nursery
Rhyme Book* © 1986 by Emily Hunter, and
The Keepsake Bible Story Coloring Book © 1993
by Emily Hunter. Used by special permission.

Printed in the United States of America.

97 98 99 00 01 02 / WZ / 10 9 8 7 6

This book belongs to

_____

From

_____

The
TABLE
OF
CONTENTS

The
VIRTUE OF
HONESTY

An HONEST person is
upright in all of his ways.
He does not take that
which does not
belong to him.
He does not pretend
to be that which
he is not.
He is genuine and true,
sincere and real.

THE MAN WHO PAID BACK
ALL HE HAD STOLEN
(Luke 19:1-10)

One day I heard a hustle
    And a bustle down the street.
I thought, "It's Jesus coming!
    He's a man I want to meet!"

What did I do? One thing I knew:
    No time was there to waste.
I ran up to a sycamore tree
    And climbed its limbs in haste.

And there came Jesus down
    the street.
He looked straight up at me.
    He said, "Zacchaeus,
You come down! Come down
    from out of that tree!"

And then what happened?
    Wondrous things!
My life was greatly blessed.
    For Jesus came to eat with me.
        He was my dinner guest.

I looked straight into Jesus' eyes
    And knew He was God's Son.
And all at once my heart felt sad
    For wrong things I had done.

I said, "I'll give back all I stole,
    And more I will repay!"
For Jesus came to my house,
And changed my heart
    that day!

THE RUINED SWEATER

Jennie Jo was naughty!
Jennie Jo was bad!
She took her sister's sweater—
The best one that she had.
She wore it to the neighbor's.
She laid it on the ground.
A puppy came and grabbed it,
And dragged it all around.
The puppy bit and chewed it.
He tossed it in the air.
And when he finished tossing it,
It wasn't fit to wear.

When Jennie's sister saw it,
She cried with all her might.
"You never should have taken it.
You know it wasn't right!"
Jennie Jo was sorry.
She said, "I know 'twas wrong!
Your sweater wasn't mine to take.
To you it did belong!
I'll never take your things again,
Except on one condition,
And that is if I ask you,
And you give me your permission!"

FORBIDDEN SWEETS

Naughty Jimmy helps himself
To candy on the grocer's shelf.
He says, "I only want to try it.
If I like it . . . then I'll buy it!"

But this is very wrong to do.
It isn't honest, right, or true.
The candy isn't his to eat
Until he's paid for his bite of sweet!

HOW FATHER MOUSE CAPTURED THE THIEF

Once upon a time in Mouse Town there lived a family of mice—Father Mouse, Mother Mouse, and their five little mice. Though Father Mouse worked hard every day to put food on the table, sometimes Mother Mouse had to put their children to bed with hollow, hungry stomachs.

One day when Mother Mouse was hanging out the laundry, Neighbor Mouse said, "Have you heard the news? There's a thief in Mouse Town! Every night he sneaks into houses and steals food!"

Mother Mouse was shocked. "Who do you think it could be?" she asked. Neighbor Mouse replied, "Some think it's Mr. Bad Mouse from the other side of town, because he sleeps in his hammock all day and never works. But no one knows for sure."

One morning when Mother Mouse went to her pantry to get

some grain, she found their grain sack gone. "The thief has come!" she cried. "He's stolen our grain!" Mother Mouse shook her head sadly for that sack of grain was precious. It would have provided many meals for her family.

The five little mice began to cry. "What will we eat?" they wailed. Mother Mouse replied, "This morning we'll have to eat dry bread. But Father gets paid today. Perhaps he'll have enough money to buy us more grain."

And Father Mouse did. He bought one sack of grain. As he placed it in the pantry, he wondered, "Will the thief return tonight?"

Then he thought of a plan to catch the thief. "He must have crawled through the pantry window," he reasoned, "so I'll place a tub of water beneath the window. If he climbs in, he'll land in the water and won't be able to get out!"

But the next morning when Father Mouse went to the pantry, he found the sack of grain gone— and so was the thief! The tub had sprung a leak and water was all over the floor. Father Mouse sadly announced, "The thief has stolen our food again!"

When Mother Mouse placed dry bread on the table once more, the five little mice began to cry. Father Mouse said, "Don't cry, children. I'll sell my gold watch. Then I'll have money to buy more grain."

No!" cried Mother Mouse. "You mustn't sell the watch your father gave you!"

But he did. And with the money, he bought another sack of grain. When Father Mouse placed the sack in the pantry, he said, "If the thief comes tonight, I'll be sure to catch him! I'll sleep right here in the pantry!"

"But how will you wake up when he comes?" asked Mother Mouse.

Father Mouse replied, "I'll tie one end of a piece of string to the grain sack, and the other end I'll tie around my finger. If the thief tries to carry off the sack, the string will tug on my finger and wake me up."

That night Father Mouse hid behind a barrel in the pantry. After tying one end of the string snugly around the sack and the other end around his finger, he went sound asleep.

Did the thief return that night? Yes, he did. But he tiptoed so quietly that Father Mouse did not hear him enter. When the thief started to lift the sack off the floor, his foot happened to be on top of the string and the string broke! The thief escaped with the sack while Father Mouse slept on and on.

The next morning when Father Mouse awoke, he looked for the grain sack. It was gone! He looked for the string. It lay broken on the floor! "The thief has won again!" he moaned.

As the five little mice nibbled their few remaining crumbs of dry bread, they begged, "Please, can we have grain tomorrow?"

"Yes!" replied Mother Mouse, "You shall have grain!" She slipped her gold wedding ring off her finger and handed it to her husband. "Take it!" she said. "Sell my wedding ring so you can buy more grain!"

"No!" replied Father Mouse. "I will not sell your wedding ring!"

But he did. For he did not want his children to go hungry.

That evening Father Mouse paced back and forth . . . thinking . . . thinking . . . thinking! Mother Mouse said, "Don't be upset, dear husband! God doesn't want that thief to keep on stealing. God will show you how to catch him!"

Father Mouse suddenly felt ashamed. He hadn't even thought of asking God to help him catch the thief. Before he went to sleep that night, Father Mouse prayed, "God, please show me how to catch the thief!" As he was drifting off to sleep, strange words came floating through his mind.

Nibble a hole . . . nibble a hole!
A hole in the sack you must eat!
Follow the grain . . . follow
the grain!
Follow the grain down
the street!

The words awoke him. He jumped out of bed. Of course! Why hadn't he thought of that before? "Thank You, God!" he said. And he ran into the pantry to nibble a hole in the bottom of the sack.

The next morning he couldn't wait to look in the pantry. His sack of grain was gone. But he searched the floor for something else. Yes! There they were! Little kernels of grain had leaked out of the hole in the sack. And they were marking a path for him to follow!

Father Mouse was excited. He slung a bundle of rope over his shoulder and started to follow the kernels of grain. Down the street he followed them . . . around a corner . . . down a hill . . . to the other side of town. At last the grain path led him to the door of an old barn beside a small house. He peered through a crack in the barn door. There on the floor he saw his grain sacks and other bundles of food.

Suddenly Father Mouse heard a low rumble. It sounded like a snore. Yes, it was a snore . . . and it was coming from a hammock in the yard beside the house. Inside the hammock lay the thief! Yes, it was Mr. Bad Mouse—just as the

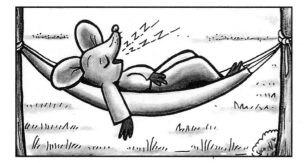

town had suspected!

Grabbing his rope tightly, Father Mouse crept toward the hammock. Then with one swift twirl, he threw his rope across Mr. Bad Mouse. Quickly he drew the rope down under the hammock and up again . . . winding it around . . . and around . . . and around . . . until Mr. Bad Mouse was completely encircled by the rope.

Mr. Bad Mouse awoke yelling and kicking! "Let me *go!*" he screamed. "Let me *go!*" He wiggled and squirmed, but he was helpless. He was tied up in his own hammock.

Father Mouse paid no attention to his screaming. He quickly cut the hammock down, doubled it into a pouch with the thief inside, and slung the hammock over his shoulder. Off he strode into town with Mr. Bad Mouse screaming inside the bundle all the way.

Everyone in Mouse Town came running out of their homes as Father Mouse walked down the street. "What's in the bag?" they hollered.

"It's the thief!" Father Mouse answered triumphantly.

"The *thief?* Hooray! The thief's

been caught! Hooray for Father Mouse!" they cheered. As Father Mouse carried the thief to the jail, the people followed him down the street like a big parade.

That night all the bundles of stolen food were returned to their owners. The five little mice went to bed with plump, contented stomachs. And that night everyone in Mouse Town slept soundly, no longer fearing the thief.

The next day the people were still talking about Father Mouse and how he had rid the town of the thief. They were so grateful for what he had done that they took up a collection of money to buy back Father Mouse's gold watch and Mother Mouse's gold wedding ring.

In a grand ceremony on the steps of the City Hall, the mayor of Mouse Town presented the watch to Father Mouse and the ring to Mother Mouse as all the people cheered and clapped. How happy Mother Mouse was to have her gold wedding ring on her finger again! How happy Father Mouse was to have his gold watch in his vest pocket again! And how happy were their five little mice who no longer had hollow, hungry stomachs.

But what happened to Mr. Bad Mouse? After many months in jail, Mr. Bad Mouse was finally allowed to return home. But Mr. Bad Mouse had learned his lesson. No longer did he sleep in his hammock all day long. Instead, Mr. Bad Mouse worked with his hands to earn money to buy his own food. In fact, he often worked so long and so hard that he was able to buy more food than he could use. And he went happily through Mouse Town giving away bags of food— oftentimes to the same families he had once stolen from. He especially liked to give food to Father Mouse and Mother Mouse because the five little mice always squealed such a big, happy thank you!

Since Mr. Bad Mouse was no longer the same bad mouse he had once been, but now was often the happiest mouse in Mouse Town, he was given a new name. Instead of calling him Mr. *Bad* Mouse, the people now called him Mr. *Glad* Mouse! And that made him very glad—just like his name.

The
VIRTUE OF
CHEERFULNESS

To practice
CHEERFULNESS
is an honorable habit.
To smile, to laugh,
to be glad, to be
joyful, brings pleasure
and delight to those
around you and
attracts blessings
into your own life, too.

HAPPYVILLE and GRUMPYTOWN

Where do happy children live?
They live in Happyville,
Where birdies sing and children swing,
And daisies dance on the hill!

The happy children smile all day.
Their faces wear no frowns.
For every child loves to obey,
And happiness abounds.

Where do grumpy children live?
  They live in Grumpytown,
    Where grumpies fret and pout and cry,
      And smiles are upside down!

Their dogs are sad, their cats are mad,
And the flowers hang their head!
For never once in Grumpytown
Is a kind word ever said!

Where do you want to live and play?
If you pout and fret and frown,
You'll have to spend the live-long day
With the grumpies in Grumpytown!

But if you choose
the happy way—and
you can, if you simply
will, then you can
smile and laugh all day,
with the children
in Happyville.

THE LITTLE BIRD'S SECRET

"I wish I were happy!" said Mindy Lou.
Then close by her side a little bird flew.
He said, "I'll tell you a secret true.
God wants you happy, and He will help you!
Upon your face, you must wear a big smile.
And you will be happy after a while."

As Mindy Lou watched the bird fly away,
She said, "I'll try it! I'll smile today!
I'll smile even though I am feeling blue.
I'll see if the little bird's secret is true!"
So Mindy Lou made her way down the street,
Smiling at all that she happened to meet.

She smiled at the neighbor mowing his grass.
He smiled as he said, "Good morning, sweet lass!"

She smiled at the widow who lived all alone.
She smiled at her dog who lay chewing a bone.

She smiled at the postman, carrying his sack.
He said, "Howdy-do!" And he smiled right back!

She smiled at wee Willie, petting his cat.
And Willie called, "Mindy! Stop and we'll chat!"

She smiled at the grandma with silver-gray hair.
She smiled at everyone everywhere!

And each time she smiled, her smile grew and grew,
Until she was smiling all through and through!

The whole world was filled with sunshine, it seemed.
For each time she smiled—right back it beamed!

Then close by her side, again the bird flew.
He asked, "Did you find that my secret was true?"

And right at that moment our sweet Mindy Lou,
Discovered, indeed, she was no longer blue!

THE PRINCE WHO NEVER SMILED

There once was a king who had a son who never smiled. As the king grew old, he realized he was soon to die and his son, the young prince, would take over his kingdom. "But what kind of a king will he be if he never smiles?" the king reasoned. "And won't his people feel sad every time they look at him?"

So the king sent out his messengers throughout all the kingdom announcing that a chest filled with gold would be given to the one who could make the young prince smile. When the people heard this, they were excited. Each one wondered, "Could I be the one to make the prince smile? Could I be the one to win the chest of gold?" One by one they eagerly sought an appearance before the prince.

First came the jester dressed in his brightly colored costume. He danced . . . he pranced . . . he made funny faces . . . but the prince did not smile.

Next came the magician. With great flourishes, he made rabbits appear and disappear from his hat.

He pulled bright balloons out of his sleeves. But the prince did not smile.

Then came the baker carrying a silver tray filled with cream puffs, tarts, and frosted cakes. He proudly presented them to the prince. But the prince did not smile.

Next came the tailor. With a grand sweep of his hand, he spread before the prince the most elegant suit of clothes ever seen in the kingdom. "These are yours!" he exclaimed. But even that did not make the prince happy enough to smile.

Over and over again, people

came before the prince. Over and over again they failed to make him smile.

What the people did not guess was that the prince wore a sober face because he thought no one really loved him. His mother had died when he was a small boy, and his father, the king, was so busy ruling his kingdom that he found no time to spend with the prince.

The hired governess who took care of the prince treated him well. "But," reasoned the prince, "she takes care of me only for the payment she receives—not because she loves me!"

When the prince rode down the street on his white horse, all the people in the kingdom bowed

and smiled. But the prince told himself, "They bow and smile only because the law of the land requires that they honor me—not because they love me!"

But no one knew that the prince felt unloved. They knew only that he never smiled. And with each person who failed to make him smile, the king grew more and more desperate. "Surely," he said, "there is someone in all my kingdom who can make my son smile!" So the king once again sent out his messengers. But this time he sent them to the farthest point of his kingdom.

In a small cottage at the border of the kingdom lived a peasant girl named Marabelle. Everyone who knew Marabelle loved her. And Marabelle loved everyone she knew. She loved every creature of the woods, every bird, every rabbit, every squirrel. She loved *all* people everywhere and *all* creatures everywhere because she loved God.

When the king's messengers arrived at Marabelle's humble cottage, she listened carefully to what they had to say. As she heard their words, her heart leaped within her, for she knew exactly what would make the prince smile.

Marabelle cried out, "Please, sirs, take me with you to the palace! I know I can make the prince smile!"

The king's messengers looked down at the peasant girl. *A poor country girl like this? they thought. With no talents? No skills? No gifts to offer? How could she possibly be the one the king is seeking?*

Reading their thoughts, Marabelle turned to her parents and pled, "Tell them, Father! Tell them, Mother! Tell them to take me to the palace. I *know* I can help the prince!"

Believing their daughter, the parents nodded to the king's messengers. And the young peasant girl was taken to the king's palace and immediately ushered into the court to appear before the prince.

Whereas all the others had made grand, flourishing entrances, Marabelle walked quietly and humbly down the royal carpet until she stood squarely before the prince. A hush fell over the room. Even in her simple peasant dress, the young maiden looked beautiful. Marabelle tilted her head upward to look directly into the prince's eyes. He returned the gaze, looking deep into Marabelle's eyes.

At last she spoke . . . softly . . . and slowly . . . but with sweet pleading in her voice. "Dear prince," she began . . .

*Heed, I pray, the words I say,
for they are very true!
God above is full of love, and He
loves me and you!*

The palace grew quiet. The prince breathed heavily as he pondered these wonderful words— words he had never before heard. *God loves me? Someone really loves me?* Every eye in the room was fastened upon the prince.

Leaning back in his chair, the prince drew a deep breath. His mouth relaxed. Suddenly his eyes lit up. Slowly over his face crept a big . . . happy . . . *smile!*

The king burst out in cheers! His messengers cheered, too! The buglers blew their bugles! Trumpets sounded! Soon the entire city was astir with the wonderful news! *"The prince has smiled! The prince has smiled!"*

All through the city, the bells rang out! All the people knew without a doubt that the prince had smiled.

That same night a great feast was held to award the chest of gold to the one who had made the prince smile. Marabelle received it humbly, and after making certain that her parents were provided for, she distributed the gold among the poor people of the kingdom.

The king soon died, and the prince took Marabelle to be his bride. They lived happily ever after, ruling over the land and encouraging all their people to love and serve God.

◆ ◆ ◆

"A MERRY HEART"

(Proverbs 17:22)

A little bird was sitting
Upon the window sill,
And looking through the window,
He smiled at little Jill.

"Little Jill," the birdie said,
"Why do you look so sad?
I'll sing a pretty song for you,
And it will make you glad!"

"Chirp, chirp! Trill, trill!"
The birdie sang a song for Jill.
"Chirp, chirp! Tweet, tweet!"
The song he sang was very sweet.

The bird looked through the window
Again at little Jill.
She said, "Oh, little birdie,
I felt so very ill.

"But you have cheered me greatly.
I know the Scriptures tell

That if I have a merry heart,
'Twill help me to get well!

"I thank the Lord in Heaven
Who has given you your song,
For now I shall feel better
The whole day long!"

The
VIRTUE OF
COURTESY

*COURTESY is
doing the kindest thing
in the kindest way,
in all that you do,
and all that you say.
To be courteous
is to be polite and
mannerly, respectful and
thoughtful of others,
thus making life
more pleasant for all.*

SELFISH TIMMY
AND THOUGHTFUL JIMMY

When Timmy entered the living room,
With Grandma close behind,
He said, "I'll grab the softest chair—
The first one that I find!"

So Timmy quickly settled down
Into the only chair,
And left his poor old grandma,
Sadly standing there.

Thoughtful little Jimmy knew
That Jesus said, "Be kind."
And so he jumped up from his chair,
And said, "Oh, please take mine!"

And poor, tired old grandma
Smiled at Jimmy happily.
She sat down in the chair—and then
Took Jimmy on her knee!

THE HAPPY BEAR FAMILY

When Papa Bear is sleeping—
Sleeping in the house,
Teddy Bear is quiet—
Quiet as a mouse.

He tiptoes very softly—
Softly on the floor,
And never beats upon his drum
Or slams the kitchen door.

When Baby Bear is napping—
Napping in her bed,
Teddy Bear won't holler,
But whispers soft instead.

He whispers to his mommy,
And to his brother, too.
For Mommy Bear has told him
That's the thoughtful thing to do.

When Papa Bear awakens
And gets up from his nap,
He smiles at little Teddy Bear
And takes him on his lap.

When Baby Bear awakens,
All rested from her sleep,
She gives her brother Teddy Bear
A kiss upon his cheek.

So all the bears are rested.
They eat a bite and talk,
And then they all go out to take
A happy family walk.

DINNER TABLE COURTESY

To the table, bring no pet.
At the table, never fret.
To the table, bring no toy
Or anything that might annoy.

Never, never come to eat
Without some shoes upon your feet.
Never sit down at your place
With dirty hands or dirty face.

Before you eat, you bow your head.
You close your eyes and pray.
You thank the Lord for all the food
He's given you today.

Keep one hand laid in your lap.
Do not slouch. Sit straight and tall.
If your mouth is full of food,
Do not laugh or talk at all.

Never reach across the table.
Simply say, "If you are able,
Will you pass the milk or cheese?
I would like some, if you please."

If you find you have to sneeze,
Always say, "Excuse me, please!"
Quickly turn your head away,
So others' food you do not spray.

Children first must always eat
All their vegetables and meat.
Then if Mother brings a treat,
They may have a bite of sweet.

THOUGHTFUL MANNERS

WHEN SHOPPING AT THE GROCERY STORE:

> When Jack is at the grocery store,
> He's happy and he's quiet.
> He never begs if Mother says
> She doesn't want to buy it!

WHEN AT SCHOOL OR CHURCH:

> Whenever Billy goes to school,
> He listens to the teacher.
> Whenever Billy goes to church,
> He listens to the preacher.
>
> He sits real quiet in his seat.
> He doesn't squirm or wiggle.
> He doesn't sneak a bite to eat.
> He doesn't joke or giggle.

WHEN FRIENDS COME TO CALL:

> When Mother's visiting with friends,
> Jill never stands between.
> For then Mother could not see her friends,
> And Mother could not be seen.

WHEN MOTHER IS SICK:

> When Mother has a headache
> And is sick in bed all day,
> Johnny, Jim, and Julie Anne
> Are quiet when they play.

WHEN EATING IN A RESTAURANT:

When Tim eats in a restaurant,
He pounds upon the table.
He bangs his spoon . . . he yells and screams
As loud as he is able.

He scatters food all over
Just like pigs eat in a pen.
His father says, "This is *enough!*
We'll *never* come again!"

When Dick eats in a restaurant,
With others eating near him,
He never yells because he knows
They wouldn't want to hear him!

He lays his napkin on his lap,
He sits up tall and straight,
And when he's done, he lays his knife
And fork across his plate.

WHEN RECEIVING A GIFT:

When someone brings a gift to Sue,
She always says a nice "thank you!"
And then she adds the person's name.
"Thank you, John!" or "Thank you, Jane!"

WHEN IT'S TIME FOR CHURCH:

When Jim and Julie go to church,
They're careful how they dress.
They clean their shoes and comb their hair,
So they will look their best.

WHEN OTHERS ARE SPEAKING:

Tammy never interrupts.
She waits till they are through.
For this is what a thoughtful child
Will always try to do.

WHEN ENTERING THE HOUSE:

Billy always wipes his feet
Before he comes indoors.
He never leaves wet, dirty tracks
Behind him on the floors.

WHEN MOTHER SAYS IT'S BEDTIME:

Sam and Suzie quickly obey.
They go to bed without delay.
They never whimper, never whine
When mother says, "It's sleepy time!"

WHEN AN ACCIDENT HAPPENS:

When Tommy steps on Cindy's toes,
Or accidentally bumps her nose,
He quickly says, "Oh, pardon me!
For I'm as sorry as can be!"

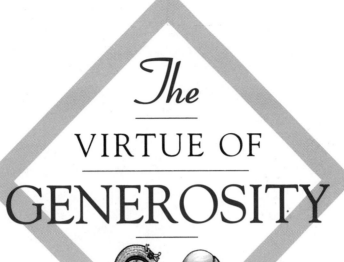

The
VIRTUE OF
GENEROSITY

To be GENEROUS
is to be willing to share
your possessions with those
around you.
To be generous is to
think of others as
well as yourself.
Generosity brings
happiness.
Selfishness does not.

THE BOY WHO SHARED HIS LUNCH

(John 6:1-14)

"Little boy, little boy!
I hesitate to ask it . . .
Little boy, could you share
Whatever's in your basket?"

"Take it, sir! Take it, sir!
It's just a tiny lunch.
With all the many people here,
It isn't very much.

"There're only five small barley loaves
And these two little fish.
My mother fixed them just for me,
But take them if you wish!"

And as the little boy looked on,
His eyes popped out of his head!
For everyone had fish to eat
And everyone had bread!

For when the Savior took his lunch,
And asked a blessing on it,
Each time a piece was broken off,
A new one grew upon it!

Yes, everyone had lots to eat.
Each person ate his fill.
And when they all could eat no more,
There were twelve baskets still!

SAD JAN

"May I swing?" asked Billy.
"May I swing?" asked Lou.
"May I swing?" asked Vicki,
"As soon as you are through?"

"It's *my* swing," said Jan,
"And no one swings but *me*!"
So back and forth she swung
   and swung
Beneath the apple tree.

"Goodbye, Jan!" said Billy.
"Goodbye, Jan!" said Lou.
"Goodbye, Jan!" said Vicki.
"We cannot play with you!"

As Jan was swinging back and forth,
Her playmates all went home.
And selfish Jan sat in her swing . . .
Just sat there all alone.

"Oh, please come back now, Billy!
Oh, please come back now, Lou!
Oh, please come back now, Vicki!
I'll share my swing with you!"

So Billy, Lou, and Vicki
Came back to swing and play,
And Jan and all her little friends
Were happy all the day.

THE WIDOW WHO SHARED HER LAST FOOD

(1 Kings 17:8-16)

Elijah asked the widow
Who was going down the street,
"Woman, can you bring me
Just a crust of bread to eat?"
The widow woman looked at him
And sadly shook her head.
"There's nothing in my house
   to eat,
Not even any bread."

"My barrel of flour is empty.
There's just a handful there.
My cooking oil is almost gone.
There's not a drop to spare.
I soon shall build a little fire
With these two sticks of wood,
And then my son and I will eat
The last bit of our food."

Elijah said, "Go make your bread, and quickly build your fire.
   But when you've baked your loaf of bread, give me what I desire.
For God has told me that He'll never let your oil run dry.
   And He has said that He will keep your flour barrel filled up high!"

The widow thought, "His word is true! I'll do what he has said!"
   She emptied all her flour and oil, and baked the man some bread.
She gave it to Elijah, and he ate it—every bite!
   But then she found more oil and flour and shouted with delight!

And though she dipped out oil and flour
          to make bread every day,
               The flour and oil did not run out!
                    They never went away!

SELFISH SUE

Selfish Sue, selfish Sue,
　　With toys of every kind,
You never share! You never share!
　　You say, "They all are mine!"

Selfish Sue with face so blue,
　　The Bible says, "Be kind!"
Share your toys with girls and boys,
　　And then your face will shine!

HOW TO HAVE TWICE THE TOYS (AND TWICE THE FUN!)

Let's walk down the street
  in Happyville,
And stop for a visit with
  little Jill.

What is Jill doing?
  Look through the door.
She's playing with brother
  On the floor.

Listen a moment . . .
  What do you hear?
Jill's speaking kindly
  To brother dear!

"Timmy," she's saying
  In voice so sweet,
"Play with my drum
  Just for a treat!"

"Thank you, Jill!
  And you take my bear!"
They had *twice* the toys!
  For they'd learned to share.

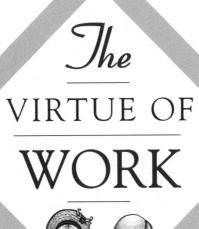

The
VIRTUE OF
WORK

When God
placed Adam
in the Garden of Eden,
He gave him WORK
to do so that
he would be
happy and busy.
Idle, lazy people
are never
happy.

THE BUSY LITTLE ANT

I'm just a tiny insect,
　　　but I'm always hard at work.
The Bible points me out
　　　to all the lazy folk who shirk.
The Bible says my ways are wise,
　　　and you will be wise, too . . .
If you follow my example
　　　in everything you do!

◆　◆　◆

WORK WITH ALL OF YOUR MIGHT

Whatever you do
　　　from morning to night,
As long as it's true . . .
　　　as long as it's right . . .
Then do what you do
　　　with all of your might!

HOW PETER MISSED A TRIP
TO THE ZOO

"Peter, Peter!
Paint my fence!
I'll gladly pay you
          50 cents!"

"No, Mr. Jones,
I can't today.
Today I want
          to run and play!"

"Peter, Peter!
Scrub my floor!
I'll pay you 20
          cents or more!"

"No, Mrs. Brown,
I can't today.
Today I want
          to run and play."

"Peter, Peter!
Weed my yard.
I'll pay you a dollar,
          for it is hard!"

"No, Mrs. Scott,
I can't today.
Today I want
          to run and play!"

"Peter, Peter, come to the zoo!
All our friends are going, too!

"Of course, you know, it isn't free.
You'll need a dollar for the fee.

"And 20 cents to feed the bear,
And 50 cents for the trolley fare!"

Peter shook his head and sighed.
"I cannot go!" the sad boy cried.

"I have no money to pay my way.
So I'll stay home alone all day!"

As Peter's friends went riding by,
He waved a sad, forlorn goodbye.

He cried, "Dear God, I'm feeling blue."
And then God showed him what to do.

He ran to the Joneses'
To paint their fence.
He worked and earned
    his 50 cents!

He went to the Browns'
To scrub their floor.
He earned his 20 cents
    and more!
He went to the Scotts'
To weed their yard.
He earned a dollar
    for it was hard!

And when his friends
Came home from the zoo,
They waved and yelled,
"We sure missed you!"
And Peter answered
With a happy glow,
"Just wait till next time!
    Then I'll go!"

IF I WERE A KITTEN

If I were a kitten, I'd eat my cream
And lie on a pillow and sleep and dream.
If I were a puppy, I'd jump and play,
And chew old shoes and bones all day.

But I am a child, so I will work.
I'll do all my tasks and never shirk.
I'll help my mother and father each day,
And then I'll go outside and play.

LAZY DAISY

Lazy Daisy was very lazy.
  She would not make her bed.
She would not put her toys away.
  She scattered them instead.

She threw her pillows on the floor.
  Her socks and dresses, too.
Her room became so full of things,
  She hardly could walk through.

But when 'twas time to go to school,
  She could not find her book.
Through piles of clothes and toys and things
  She had to look and look!

She could not find her jacket!
  She could not find her sweater!
At last she said, "I'll clean my room.
  A tidy room is better!"

"A STITCH IN TIME SAVES NINE"

"Dear me!" cried Bess, "I've ripped my dress!
      My seam's popped open. The stitches are broken.
And I must wear this dress tonight!
      My other dresses would not be right!"

"It's quick to mend," said a helpful friend.
      "You don't need to pin it. 'Twill mend in a minute!"
"Oh, no!" said Bess with a toss of her head.
      "I won't mend it now—but later instead!"

As Bess played around the rest of the day,
      The stitches continued to rip away.
The rip in her dress didn't stay the same,
      But bigger and bigger it quickly became.

Before she knew it, 'twas time for the party.
      She said, "Oh, dear! I mustn't be tardy!
Now, where is that tear to mend in a minute?
      Oh, look at it now! It's too big to pin it!"

So Bess started stitching.
      She mended and mended.
But when she was finished,
      The party had ended.
She cried, "If I'd just stitched it
      When it was small!
I wouldn't have missed
      The party at all!"

"HASTE MAKES WASTE"

"I must hurry!" said the choo-choo—and it ran right off the track.
"I must hurry!" said the turtle—and it flipped upon its back.
"I must hurry!" said the baker—and he dropped his sack of flour.
"I must hurry!" said the clock—and it skipped a half an hour.
"I must hurry!" said the banker—and he spilled a bag of gold.
Whatever else does haste do? The half has not been told!

"BUILD YOUR OWN FIRE AND IT WILL WARM YOU TWICE!"

"I'm cold!" said Bill. "Just feel my nose!
My hands are freezing and so are my toes!"
Said brother Jim, "I'm freezing, too!
But there's one thing we both can do!

"We can build a fire. Come gather wood!"
But Bill replied, "I know I should,
But I am staying in this spot,
And here I'll stay 'till the fire is hot!"

So Jim searched all the neighborhood.
He gathered sticks. He chopped up wood.
He carried chunks—a heavy load—
Huffing and puffing down the road.

He worked so hard he began to perspire,
Even before he'd built his fire.
But when he returned to brother Bill,
He found him shivering from the chill.

Huddled stiff in the corner stood he,
As cold and miserable as one could be.
But Jim's hard work made him warm as toast.
Now whom do you think the fire warmed most?

The
VIRTUE OF
COMPASSION

*To be COMPASSIONATE
is to take pity on
those in need,
to offer sympathy to
those in trouble,
to be tenderhearted toward
those who are hurting . . .
and above all
to look for ways
to show kindness and
to be helpful.*

THE
GOOD SAMARITAN
(Luke 10:30-37)

Listen, my little children dear!
    Listen to me, and you will hear
A story that Jesus told one day
    About a man who went his way
To Jericho down a lonely road.
    He was all alone, so he quickly
      strode,
For robbers were known to hide
    nearby
In the rocky hills, all barren
    and dry.
And sure enough, as the sun went
    down,
The man heard a noise and
    looked around.
And what he saw made him gasp
    in shock,
For jumping right out from
    behind a rock
Were robbers waving their clubs
    in the air!
They grabbed him, beat him,
    and stripped him bare!
Then taking his money, the
    robbers all fled,
Leaving the man in the road
    half-dead.

But as he lay groaning, the man
    heard a sound—
Somebody's footsteps upon the
    dry ground.
"Please come and help me!" the
    poor man cried.
But the traveler went by on the
    opposite side.
Soon the man heard another
    walk by.
But this traveler, too, left the
    man there to die.

"No one will stop!" the wounded
    man said.
"They all pass by. I soon shall
    be dead!"
But as he lay there in pain
    and fear,
Again he heard footsteps
    drawing near.
Closer and closer the foot-
    steps came,
Right to the spot where the
    man lay in pain.
And then the man saw a
    kind face above,
And heard a soft voice that
    was filled with love.
"I want to help you," the
    kind voice said.
"Let me pour oil on your
    bleeding head.

And on my donkey, I'll give
    you a ride,
While I walk along on the
    road by your side.
We'll go to an inn for rest and
    for sleep.
Your money's all gone, so
    I'll pay your keep."
And every kind word that the
    man spoke was true.
He did all the kind things he
    said he would do.
What a good neighbor the man
    was that day
While others selfishly went on
    their way!
And now Jesus says to me
    and to you,
"I want you to be good
    neighbors, too!"

POOR MRS. JONES

Poor Mrs. Jones
    Can walk no more.
But she needs food
    From the corner store.
She's old and weak.
    Her legs are lame.
She cannot walk
    Without a cane.

"Should I go help her?
    Of course, I should!"
Said little Mary,
    So kind and good.
And so she ran
    With her two strong legs.
And brought Mrs. Jones
    Some bread and eggs.

If Jesus came to our neighborhood,
    He'd visit the widow down the street
And take her some food so she could eat.
    So I'll help those in my neighborhood.
        If Jesus would, I know I should!

POOR MR. BROWN

Poor Mr. Brown.
    He's tired and old.
He needs a fire.
    His house is cold.
But he's too tired
    To gather wood.
"Should I go help him?
    Of course, I should!

I'll fill his wood box
    Best I can!"
Said helpful, happy
    Little Dan.
And that's exactly
    What he did.
He filled his wood box
    To the lid.

If Jesus came to our neighborhood,
    He'd be so helpful, kind, and good.
He'd take Mr. Brown some kindling wood.
    So I'll help those in my neighborhood.
        If Jesus would, I know I should!

THE WOMAN AND HER WOODPILE

The woman by the woodpile
   began to cry.
A boy walked by and asked
   her why.
"I'm crying because I'm tired,"
   she said,
"And I must put this wood in
   the shed!
I've worked and worked 'till
   I'm almost dead,
And still this pile is as tall as
   my head!

If you wish to stay, you may be
   my guest,
But I must go back to my house
   to rest."

The boy looked on as she
   trudged away,
But he didn't sit down and he
   didn't stay.
He rushed to the village as fast
   as he could.
To tell his friends of the
   woman and her wood.

"Come!" he cried. "Let's give
   her a hand!"
And soon he was followed by a
   happy band.
Children short—and children
   tall!
They marched to the woodpile
   one and all!

When the woman awoke from
   her nap, she said,
"Now I'll try to put that wood
   in the shed!"
But lo! The woodpile was no
   longer there!
The children had stacked it
   away with care.
"Oh, how did you do it?" the
   woman cried.

"It was no big task," the
children replied.
"We each took our turn! We each
carried one!
And before we knew it, the job
was all done!"
The old woman cried, "You're a
wonderful group!
Do come right in!
I'll make you some soup!"

The children all gathered around
her table,
And helped her as much as
they were able.
They peeled the carrots, they
shelled the peas,
They did whatever they could
to please.
At last they all were ready
to eat,
So each one stood beside
his seat.

The woman said, "Now it's
time to pray,
And thank the Lord for our
food today."

And while each person bowed
his head,
She thanked the Lord for their
soup and bread.
She thanked Him, too, for sending
her way
The children who stacked all her
wood that day!

When the children went home to
bed that night,
Their bodies were tired, but their
spirits were bright.
For they knew they had done
what was noble and good
When they helped the old woman
stack her load of wood.

"They helped everyone his neighbor"—Isaiah 41:6.

"Having compassion one of another"—1 Peter 3:8.

MOTHER,
WHAT CAN I DO FOR YOU?

"Mother, what can I do for you?"
Asked little Robin Redbreast.
"I'll bring you breakfast on a tray,
So you can get some bed rest!"

"Mother, what can I do for you?"
Asked Pussy Lillie Lou.
"I'll peel some vegetables and make
A kettle full of stew!"

"Mother, what can I do for you?"
Asked Melanie the Mouse.
"I'll dust and sweep the dirty floors,
And tidy up the house!"

"Mother, I just want to sit!"
Said Grouchy Kangaroo.
And so he didn't help a bit,
But sat the whole day through.

Now tell me, children, who do you think was happiest that day?
The lazy kangaroo or those who helped in every way?

THE FOX WHO SHOWED NO MERCY

A bear who was walking
    in the woods one day
Got caught in a trap
    and couldn't get away.
A fox saw the bear, and he
    laughed with delight.
"I never liked that bear!
    It serves him right!"
The bear cried, *"Help!*
    Set me free or I'll die!"
A lion heard him cry and said,
    "Yes, I'll try!"
But the fox said, "Lion, he's a
    very stupid bear!
Or he wouldn't get caught!
    He deserves to stay there!"
The lion answered, "Fox,
    I believe what you say!"
So he said, "Sorry, bear!"
    And he went on his way.
The bear cried louder,
    "Set me free or I'll die!"
A rabbit hopping by said,
    "Yes! I'll try!"
But the fox said, "Rabbit,
    you'll be eaten by that bear!
So you'd better be smart
    and just leave him there!"
The rabbit said, "Fox,
    I believe what you say!"
So he said, "Sorry, bear!"
    And he went on his way.

Then the mean old fox
    grinned from ear to ear,
Shouting, "Goodbye, bear!
    I'm leaving you here!"
As the fox went his way,
    he tripped and he fell
Right down to the bottom
    of a deep, deep well!
The fox yelled, *"Throw me*
    a rope or I'll die!"
The lion heard him yell
    and said, "My, my, my!
Mr. Fox, I believe you're
    as stupid as that bear.
So, just like the bear,
    you deserve to stay there!"
The fox heard the rabbit
    come hopping nearby,
And he yelled, "Oh, rabbit!
    Please help me or I'll die!"
The rabbit said, "No, you might
    eat me like the bear,
So I'd better be smart and just
    leave you there!"
Though the fox yelled and
    yelled, as far as we can tell . . .
He is still right there . . .
    in the *bottom of the well!*

COMPASSIONATE CLIFFORD

Clifford Green's mother always told him that he should help anyone in trouble. "It's the right thing to do," she said, "and if you help *others*, you'll be a happier boy *yourself!*"

One morning on his way to school, Cliff came upon a little boy crying. He knew immediately that the boy was lost, for he had often seen him playing outside his home many blocks away. Cliff comforted him. "Don't cry, little boy! I'll take you home!" Holding his hand, Cliff led him down the many blocks to his home. When the boy saw his home, he ran happily up to the steps crying, "Mama! Mama!" When the mother opened the door, Cliff turned to hurry back to school, for it was growing late.

His class had already begun when he arrived. "You are *very* tardy, Clifford!" said his teacher. "Do you have a written excuse?"

"No, Mrs. Lee," he replied. Then he told her about the boy. "My mother has always told me to help anyone in trouble," he explained. "It was something I had to do."

"I understand," replied Mrs. Lee. Later she handed him a note to give to his mother.

When Cliff's mother opened the note, she read it aloud:

Dear Mrs. Green: I want to commend you for teaching Clifford to help those in trouble. He went out of his way this morning to take a lost child home. I am very proud of him.

Cliff's mother gave him a hug. "I'm proud of you, too!" she said. Suddenly Cliff felt strangely good inside. He felt very, very happy! Then he realized it was just like his mother had told him:

"If you help others, you'll be a happier boy yourself!"

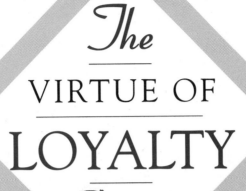

The
VIRTUE OF
LOYALTY

To be LOYAL is to be faithful
and true to those who deserve
our loyalty—
our family, our friends,
our country, and our God.
To be loyal is never to fail them,
never to speak ill of them
behind their backs,
never to desert them
when others turn against them,
but to remain
steadfast and true.

SAD, SAD PETER

(Luke 22:56-62)

Peter told Jesus he would always be His true friend, but Jesus said, "Before the rooster crows three times tomorrow morning, you will say you don't even know Me!" Peter replied, "No, Lord, I would never do that!" But that very night Peter denied the Lord. What did he do then?

It's early in the morning.
　　Children are sleeping.
Where is Peter?
　　Peter is weeping!

Why is he weeping?
　　Because the cock crew,
Cock-a-doodle-doo!
　　Cock-a-doodle-doo!

Peter heard the rooster
　　Crowing at the sun.
Then he remembered
　　The things he had done.

He had failed his Lord.
　　He had left His side.
He had cursed and sworn.
　　He had even lied.

Sad, sad Peter,
　　Weeping for his sin,
Looked across at Jesus,
　　And Jesus looked at him.

Jesus' heart was sad,
　　But Jesus still forgave him.
For Jesus came to earth
　　　　To die so He could save him.
　　Never once again
　　　　Did Peter fail his Friend.
　　He gave his life to Jesus, and
　　　　Served Him to the end.

HOW LAURA LEARNED A LESSON ABOUT LOYALTY

It was Laura's twelfth birthday. But Laura knew there would be no celebration. Her father was dead, and her mother was handicapped. Though her mother could walk, each step was painful for her. She could not control her leg movements, and her body twisted from side to side.

Laura did not know what had caused her mother to be handicapped. Whenever she asked, her mother would reply, "Someday I will tell you, Laura."

This was not only Laura's twelfth birthday, it was also her first day in a new school, for they had just moved to a new town. Laura dressed with special care that morning. She wanted to make a good impression on her new classmates so they would want to be her friends.

Laura kissed her mother goodbye and headed down the street. The school was just a few blocks away. With each step she grew more anxious. She entered the door feeling timid and shy. Soon she relaxed, however, for the teacher was kind and the girls seemed very friendly.

The morning passed quickly. When lunchtime came, several girls invited Laura to eat with them. After lunch the girls said, "We have a few minutes before class. Let's go outside in the sunshine." As they stepped out of the building, one of the girls stared hard at someone across the street. "Look!" she whispered. "Look at that funny woman over there! Look at how she walks! Have you ever seen anyone so odd?" The girls all turned their heads to stare at the woman.

One quick glance told Laura it was her mother. Her heart sank. Quickly she ducked into the shadow of the building. *What if her mother should see her and wave to her? How embarrassed she would be! What would her new friends think if they knew this was her mother? And what was her mother doing walking down the street?* The bell rang. Laura was relieved to return to her classroom.

After school Laura hurried home. As she opened the door, her mother called out, "Happy birthday, Laura!" There on the table lay a beautiful birthday cake with 12 candles on it. Laura stared in unbelief. "Where did you get the cake, Mother?"

"I walked to the store to get it!" she proudly replied. "I wanted your twelfth birthday to be a special one!"

"Oh, Mother!" Laura cried. "How can I ever thank you? But how did you manage to walk that far when it's so painful for you?" Then Laura remembered how she had hid in the shadows as her mother passed by her school. "I don't deserve a wonderful mother like you!" she sobbed.

Laura and her mother ate their cake quietly. Finally, Laura spoke. "Mother," she began, "you've al-ways said that someday you would tell me how you became handicapped. I'm 12 years old now. Do you think this might be the right time?"

Her mother nodded. "Yes, Laura," she answered, "it is the right time." Then she proceeded to tell a story that made tears flow down Laura's cheeks.

"I was injured in an accident when you were just a toddler," she said. "You were playing safely in our front yard behind a fence. But when the postman came to deliver our mail, he forgot to shut the gate behind him. A few minutes later, I looked out the kitchen window. I was horrified to see you toddling across the street! And a car was coming around the corner! I dashed out of the house just in time to push you out of the path of the car. But I could not escape the car's wheels."

Laura clung to her mother, sobbing hard. "Oh, Mother dear!" she cried. "You risked your life to save me! I might not have been here today if it weren't for your courage and love!"

"Don't cry, my precious daughter!" her mother said, as she smoothed Laura's hair. "I would gladly do it again! Many times I've thanked God that I looked out the window in time to rescue you!"

The next day Laura invited her friends to come home with her after school. "I want you to meet the most wonderful mother in the world!" she said. "You have already seen my mother, but I was too embarrassed to acknowledge her. She is the handicapped woman you saw yesterday walking down the street!" The girls let out a short gasp. "It was wrong of me to keep silent," explained Laura. "I should have been proud to claim her as my mother!" Then Laura told them the story of her mother's love and courage.

The girls' eyes grew large as they listened. Their hearts were deeply touched. When they met Laura's mother later that afternoon, she no longer appeared odd in their eyes. Instead they viewed her with deep admiration and respect.

From that day forward the girls often stopped by to visit with Laura's mother. They loved to show her small kindnesses. They delighted in bringing her flowers. They begged to run errands for her. Laura's home became a popular gathering spot for her friends. Laura was happy to share her mother with them, for she declared, "No one could be more proud of a mother than I am!"

ABSALOM, THE SON WHO PLOTTED AGAINST HIS FATHER, THE KING

(2 Samuel 18:9-15)

King David's son was Absalom—
A wicked son was he.
For Absalom was vain and proud.
He bragged, "Just look at me!"

He let his hair grow thick and long.
He said, "Don't I look fine!
No other man in all the land
Has hair as long as mine!"

Now Absalom, this wicked son,
Desired his father's throne.
And so he overthrew the king
And he was king alone.

King David's men came chasing him.
As on his mule he fled,
He didn't see the oak tree
Which was spreading out ahead.

A heavy branch was hanging low.
It caught him by his hair.
The mule ran off, and Absalom
Was left a-hanging there!

Foolish, foolish Absalom!
The hair that was his pride
Now held him for his enemies,
And that is how he died.

SHADRACH, MESHACH, AND ABEDNEGO—LOYAL TO THEIR GOD!

(Daniel 3:1-30)

King Nebuchadnezzar
  was a mighty king of old.
He made a great image and
  he covered it with gold.

He said to all the people,
  "When you hear the
  trumpets sound,
You must kneel before the
  image!
You must all bow down!"

But Shadrach and Meshach
  and young Abednego
Said, "No, we won't!
  We won't bow down!
  No . . . No . . . No!

We'll worship no one
  but our God!
We'll worship Him alone!"
And so into the furnace
  they were quickly
  thrown.

The furnace was made hotter
  than it ever was before.
It even burned the men up
  who threw them
  through the door.

The king came near the furnace
  just to see what he could see.
He knew an awful thing would
  surely happen to those three.

The sight he saw was
　　different though.
The king was all amazed!
For four men were walking
　　in the furnace as he gazed.

"The fourth one—he is different!
　　Like a Son of God!"
　　he said.
"And all the three are still alive!
　　But they should all be dead!"

The king hollered,
　　"Men, come out!
　　You men, come here to me!"
And when the men came
　　walking out,
The king could plainly see . . .

The fire had never scorched
　　their clothes,
　　or even singed their hair.
The flames had never touched
　　the men,
Or burned them anywhere!

And then the king said,
　　"Shadrach, Meshach,
　　Abednego,
Your God has saved you all
　　this day!
You men are free to go!

"Your God has sent His angel
　　to help you in your need.
There's not a God like your God!
　　He's marvelous, indeed!"

"In God have I put my trust: I will not be afraid
what man can do unto me"—Psalm 56:11.

"Our God whom we serve is able to deliver us
from the fiery furnace"—Daniel 3:17.

The
VIRTUE OF
TRUTHFULNESS

*Honorable
people
tell the TRUTH
at all times.
They neither
lie nor exaggerate.
It may take courage
to always tell the truth,
but it is always
the best way.*

CASSIDY O'TOOLE

Cassidy, Cassidy,
Cassidy O'Toole
Didn't like to study,
And he didn't like school.

He woke up on a morning
When the sun was shining bright,
And said, "This is a perfect day
To fly my purple kite!"

"Mother dear, Mother dear!"
Cassidy cried.
"I cannot go to school today,"
The naughty boy lied.

"I must have eaten too much pie
And eaten too much cake,
For I am feeling very bad
And have a stomachache!"

"Cassidy, Cassidy!
Now you must stay in bed.
And you shall have no breakfast
But a crust of dry bread.

"And here's some nasty medicine
That tastes so very sour,
And here are bitter pills to swallow
One every hour."

"Mother dear, Mother dear!"
Cassidy pled.
"I think I'm feeling better.
See! My cheeks are turning red!

"Perhaps I'd better go to school
And study very hard,
And then when I come home,
I'll fly my kite out in the yard!"

"Cassidy, Cassidy!
It's very plain to see
That you were really never sick.
You played a trick on me!

"Now I shall have to punish you
For such a naughty deed.
As soon as you get home from school,
The garden you must weed!"

"Mother dear, Mother dear!"
Cassidy cried.
"I'm sorry that I tricked you.
I'm sorry that I lied!

"It's right that I be punished
So I'll grow up to be good,
And so I'll always go to school
And do the things I should."

"Cassidy, Cassidy,
Your words are very true.
I love you and forgive you, dear,
And Jesus does, too.

"But still the garden you must weed
For punishment today,
But after school tomorrow,
You may fly your kite and play."

TOMMY TAGGER

Little Tommy Tagger
  Was a boaster and a bragger.
He told all his friends
   that he could fly.

He toppled off a ladder,
  And landed in a splatter!
And all his friends knew
   Tommy told a lie!

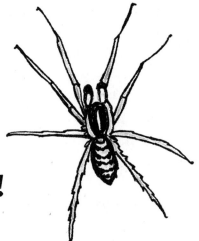

HELP! A BIG SPIDER!

"Help! A big spider!" Melody cried.
  Friends came running to Melody's side.
   They brushed off the spider
    Before it could bite her,
     For everyone knew that she never lied!

TIMOTHY GIBBS

Timothy Gibbs told so many fibs,
That no one could ever believe him.
He choked on some pie
And yelled, "Help! Or I'll die!"
But nobody came to relieve him!

THE BOY WHO LIKED TO TEASE

Jimmy was a teaser.
He played a little game.
He yelled and told his mother
That the kitchen was aflame.

She ran into the kitchen
And her heart was pounding wild.
But when she saw it wasn't true,
She said, "Oh, dearest child . . .

"Jesus wants us to be true
In every word we say,
And never, never tell a lie—
Not even just in play!"

When Jimmy's mother told him this,
He quickly bowed his head,
And prayed, "Dear Lord, forgive me
For the untrue words I said.

"And help me, please, from day to day
The truth to always speak."
Then Jimmy's mother hugged him close
And kissed him on the cheek.

WOULD YOU TELL A LIE FOR A DIME?

(Adapted from a narrative in "The Beautiful Tree of Life," 1892)

"Would you tell a lie for a dime?" said he.
"No, I wouldn't, sir!" said she.
"Would you tell a lie for a dollar?" said he.
"No, I wouldn't, sir!" said she.
"Would you lie for a hundred dollars?" said he.
"No, I wouldn't, sir!" said she.
"Would you lie for a thousand dollars then?"
"No, sir, never!" she said again.

"Then tell me, Miss, why not, I pray?"
And the old man heard the sweet miss say,
"I must not lose my honest name,
Nor bring my parents pain or shame.
And when the dollars are spent in vain,
That sinful lie would still remain."

WHEN BOBBY LIED

They all were happy till Bobby lied.
Then Daddy spanked
And Mommy sighed.
When Bobby lied, no one was glad,
And God in heaven was very sad.

The
VIRTUE OF
FRIENDSHIP

A FRIEND is someone
you enjoy being with,
someone who shares your fun,
your good times
and your bad times . . .
someone who is kind and helpful.
Everyone needs a friend,
but in order to make a friend,
you must be a friend.

THE SICK MAN'S FOUR FRIENDS

(Luke 5:18-26; Mark 2:3-12)

The sick man lay upon his bed.
    He could not move at all.
He could not walk, for if he tried,
    he knew that he would fall.

He yearned to go see Jesus,
    for he had heard men tell
That Jesus could just speak a word
    and make a sick man well.

"We'll help you!" said the sick
    man's friends.
"We'll take you there!"
    they said.
"The four of us will carry you,
    As you lie on your bed."

The sick man was so grateful,
    that he shed a happy tear.
And as they took him down
    the street,
His heart was filled with cheer.

But when they came where
    Jesus was,
The crowd was thick outside.
They could not even reach
    the door,
No matter how they tried.

"Oh, woe is me!"
    the sick man cried.
    He sadly shook his head.
"I cannot get to Jesus.
    I may as well be dead!"

"Now don't you cry,
    and don't give up,"
    His faithful friends all pled.
"Although we can't
    get through the door,
We'll try the roof instead!"

Go through the roof? Who ever heard
    of such a thing as that?
"We'll tear the roof apart and let
    you down upon your mat!"

And sure enough, that's what
    they did,
    and with their work complete,
With ropes they let him down
    until he lay at Jesus' feet.

What happened then as men
    looked on and heard the
    Savior talk?
They heard him tell the sick man,
    "Take up your bed and *walk!*"

What did he do—that sick man?
    Who could not move at all?
Who could not even try to walk
    Because he knew he'd fall?

That sick man jumped up
    on his feet with
Strength he'd never known,
    and lifting up his bed mat,
    he headed toward his home.

And as he went, he praised the
    Lord, his shining face aglow!
Now he could walk on
    two strong legs
        Where'er he chose to go!

"A friend in need is a friend indeed"—An old English proverb.

JOHNNY'S WISE CHOICE

Johnny Boy was home alone—
All alone was he.
"Oh," he said, "I'm lonely!
Lonely as can be!

"How I wish I had a friend—
Someone I could play with.
Mother's gone away and I
Have no one I can stay with!"

Then he heard a quiet knock—
A rap upon the door.
And standing there to greet him
Was his neighbor, Tommy Moore.

Now Tommy was a rowdy boy
Who always was in trouble.
And there he stood in overalls,
And in his hand a shovel.

He said, "Come out and play with me.
We both can have some sport.
I've got a really great idea.
We'll build ourselves a fort.

"And then we'll shoot my BB gun
At people walking by!
Of course, we'll be real careful not
To hit them in the eye!"

"Tommy Moore!" said Johnny Boy.
"That is no way to play!
Although it's very lonely here,
Alone I'd rather stay . . .

"Than enter into sport with you
In such a naughty way!
And so to you, my Tommy Moore,
I'll simply say, 'Good day!' "

" 'Tis better to be alone than in bad company"—George Washington.

HOW "SLOWPOKE JOE" WON A FRIEND

"Mother, Mother!" called Joe as he rushed home from school. "I'm going to win a pair of skates—just what I've always wanted!"

"You are?" his mother asked, looking puzzled.

"Well . . ." he stammered. "I'm going to try, anyway. I'm entering the school race, and the prize is a pair of skates. But, Mother, I *know* I can win! I'm going to practice *hard!*"

Joe's mother smiled. "I wish you luck," she replied, "but some other boy might practice hard, too."

A shadow spread across Joe's face. Everyone knew that Sylvester Snyder was the fastest runner in the school. Everyone knew he was also the *meanest* boy in the school—and the *richest*—for his dad owned the town mill. Joe recalled how just that morning Sylvester had kicked him in the shins as they passed in the hall. *"So you're entering the race, are you? Ho, ho, ho! 'Slowpoke Joe' is entering a race!"* But Joe paid no

attention to Sylvester's sneering remarks. He was determined to win the race—*and the skates!*

Day after day Joe practiced running. When everyone else was playing ball or swimming, Joe was practicing . . . practicing . . . practicing! And as he practiced, his muscles grew stronger, and his endurance grew greater. When the day of the race came, Joe was in excellent shape.

Many people in the community came to watch the race. Joe's parents were there, and Sylvester's, too. As Joe took his position at the starting line, Sylvester sneered at him, "Ho, ho, ho! 'Slowpoke Joe'! Running a race!" But Joe closed his ears to Sylvester's taunts. Instead he waited, poised and tense for the starting signal.

There it was! He was off! Running smoothly . . . running skillfully! He caught sight of Sylvester beside him. It was a close race.

First Joe was ahead . . . then Sylvester . . . then they were neck and neck with the others not far behind! But as they continued

running, Joe saw that he was gradually inching ahead. Sylvester was no longer able to keep up with him. *I'm winning the race!* Joe thought. In his mind's eye, he could see himself receiving the pair of skates!

But now the racetrack was curving through a stretch of thick woods. The crowd's cheering died down, for the runners were now completely out of sight.

Joe heard a thud behind him. He glanced around. There on the track lay Sylvester Snyder holding one leg and writhing in pain! He

had stumbled and fallen. Everyone else was running on ahead, but Joe slowed down. For one brief moment he thought, *"What shall I do?"* Then he *knew*. He knew exactly what he should do.

Back at the grandstand, Joe's parents were puzzled. Other runners were coming into sight around the bend of the woods. *But where was Joe? Where was Sylvester? Surely they would come in ahead of the others.* Just then a loud cheer went up from the crowd. Joe's parents turned to see a runner crossing the finish line. "Oh, dear!" they thought. "Someone else has won the skates!"

A few minutes later Joe appeared around the bend of the track. He was trudging slowly, supporting Sylvester over one shoulder. Sylvester was trying to hobble along. But it was evident that every step caused him great pain. Joe raised his eyes to the grandstand just in time to see the winner receiving the prize—the skates he had dreamed of having!

It was all over. Joe went quietly home. Was he disappointed? Of course. But somehow he felt good inside, for he knew he had done the right thing. As mean as Sylvester had been to him, he still couldn't leave him suffering there alone, out of sight, with no one to help him.

Several days later there was a knock at his door. His mother called out, "Joe, someone to see you!" Joe entered the living room to find Sylvester and his father standing there. Sylvester was leaning on crutches. Mr. Snyder held out a package toward Joe.

"Open it," he said. "It's for you."

As Joe lifted the lid of the box, his mouth flew open in surprise.

There before him lay a beautiful pair of silver skates!

Mr. Snyder said, "This is what you would have won if you hadn't stopped to help my son. I thank you!"

"I thank you, too," added Sylvester shyly, "and I want to be your friend—if you can forgive me!" Joe reached out and grabbed Sylvester's hand, beaming happily.

That night Joe went to bed thankful for his new skates, but even more thankful for his new friend. When his parents told him goodnight, they said, "Son, in our eyes you are not a loser . . . you are a true winner!"

TO HAVE FRIENDS . . . BE FRIENDLY!

How do friendly children speak
Whenever they're at play?
They're kind to one another
In every word they say.

You hear them saying, "Thank you!"
You hear them saying, "Please."
You hear them saying, "Let's take turns."
You never hear them tease.

How do hateful children act
Whenever they're at play?
They call bad names, they criticize
With every word they say.

They stomp their feet. They holler.
They're sassy and they're cross.
And each and every one of them
Declares that he is boss!

---

*"He that hath friends must show himself
friendly"—Proverbs 18:24.*

The
VIRTUE OF
THANKFULNESS

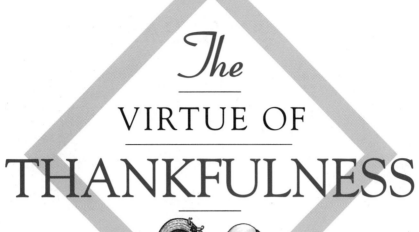

*A spirit
of gratitude
shows a good heart.
It is always right
to express appreciation
for kindnesses
shown to you
or for gifts received.
Above all else,
remember to say
"THANK YOU"
to God.*

HOW BUNNY JAKE BAKED A CAKE

There once was a bunny
    By the name of Jake.
One day he said,
    "What shall I make?

"I know what I'll make.
    I'll make a cake,
And put it in the oven
    To bake and bake."

But then the bunny
    By the name of Jake
Said, "What will I need
    To make my cake?

"I'll need some butter
    And I'll need some milk,
And I'll need some flour
    That is soft as silk.
I'll need some eggs,
    And I'll need some honey."
So off went the happy little bunny.

He hopped away on his little legs
    To the chicken house to get two eggs.

The hen said, "I've laid eggs for you.
For God has said that's what I'm to do!"
"Thank you, hen!" said Bunny Jake.
"These eggs will help me make my cake!"

He went to the miller
That very same hour,
And said, "Can you grind
Some grain into flour?"
The miller said, "Yes,
I have lots of grain,
For God sent the sun,
And He sent the rain."
"Thank you, miller!"
Said Bunny Jake,
"This flour will help me
Make my cake!"

And then he went to some busy bees.
He said, "Can you spare some
    honey, please?"
"Yes," said the bees,
"That's within our power,
For God puts sweetness
    in each flower!"
"Thank you, bees!" said Bunny Jake.
"This honey will help me
    make my cake!"

He went to the cow
With her big round udder.
He said, "Please give me
Some milk and butter."
The cow said, "Yes,
I can fill your need,
For God's given grass
On which I feed.
My milk is rich.
You can take the cream
And make the best butter
You've ever seen!"

"Thanks for the milk
And the butter," said Jake.
"Dear cow, you've helped me
Make my cake!"

And then the bunny by the name of Jake
Had all he needed to make his cake.
He had his butter. He had his milk.
He had his flour ground soft as silk.
He had all the honey that he might need,
And two big eggs that were fresh indeed.

He mixed and mixed and stirred and stirred,
And then without another word,
He put it in the oven so it could bake,
And after a while . . . *out came a cake!*

He called to his friends,
   "You come and eat!
Just see what I've made!
   A cake so sweet!"
When Jake's good friends
   All came to see,
The proud bunny said,
   "Just look at me!
Who else in the world
   But great Bunny Jake
Could be so great
   As to make this cake!"

But as the bunny was
   Puffed with pride,
Just who do you think
   Ran up to his side?
Here came the miller
   And the cow, if you please!
Here came the hen!
   And here came the bees!

They said, "We heard you,
   Bunny Jake!
We heard you bragging
   About your cake!
But we want all your
   Friends to know
'Twas God who made
   The grain to grow!
God gave the cow
   Her milk and cream.
God gave the grass she ate,
   So green.
God gave the bees
   The flowers so sweet,
And God gave the hens
   The eggs we eat!"

When Jake heard all
    The words they said,
He answered, "Friends,
    Let's bow our head.
Before we even
    Take one bite,
Let's thank the Lord,
    For this is right!"

And all Jake's friends
    Who gathered there,
Bowed heads and closed
    Their eyes in prayer.
"We thank You, God!"
    Prayed Bunny Jake.
And then his friends
    All ate their cake!

MY "THANK-YOU" NOTE TO GOD

I wrote a "thank you" note today
To my dear Grandma Lee,
To thank her for the birthday gift
That she had sent to me.

And then I thought of all the gifts
That God has given me.
He's given me the food I eat
And everything I see!

And so I wrote a "thank-you" note
To God in heaven above,
And signed it, *"From your little child,
Rebecca Jane, with love!"*

A DAY TO GIVE THANKS

"It is a good thing to give thanks unto the LORD" (Psalm 92:1).

Everyone's here!
There's laughter and
    chatter!
Out in the kitchen
Dishes a-clatter!
See the big turkey!
If it were fatter,
It wouldn't fit on
Mother's big platter!

Now we're all seated
Next to each other.
Dad's at the head,
I'm next to brother.
Next comes my sis,
And then my dear
    mother.
(Oh, she is sweet!
Oh, how I love her!)

Everything's ready!
The table is spread!
Everyone's still.
We each bow our head.
We thank God for
    blessings!
We thank Him for bread!
And now we all eat,
For the blessing is said!

HERE IS NED

Here is Ned—
     Good little Ned!
Before he eats,
     He bows his head,
And though he's hungry
     For his bread,
He takes not a bite
     Till the blessing is said.

"Be thankful unto him"—Psalm 100:4.

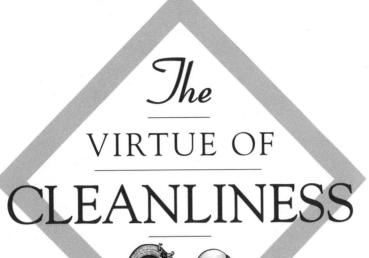

The

VIRTUE OF

CLEANLINESS

Our bodies
are given to us
by God.
We honor this gift
by taking good care of them.
This not only means keeping
them CLEAN, but also doing
nothing to harm or injure them.
We honor our bodies by
clothing them in
neat, clean
garments.

THIS IS THE WAY

This is the way we wash our face.
God wants us to be clean.
This is the way we brush our teeth
To make them shine and gleam.

This is the way we comb our hair.
God wants us to be neat.
This is the way we dress ourselves.
Now don't we look real sweet!

This is the way we talk to God
Upon our knees in prayer.
We tell Him that we love Him
And we thank Him
for His care.

THREE MUDDY PIGS

Three scrubbed pigs!
  Three scrubbed pigs!
See how they shine!
  See how they shine!
The farmer washed them so very clean.
  They shimmer and sparkle
  And shine and gleam!
Did you ever see any pigs so clean
  As three scrubbed pigs!
  Three scrubbed pigs!

Three muddy pigs!
  Three muddy pigs!
No longer clean.
  No longer clean.
As soon as the farmer set them free,
They all got as dirty as dirty can be!
They love to be dirty, it's easy to see.
  Three muddy pigs!
  Three muddy pigs!

HOW SAMMY NELSON GOT A JOB

Sammy Nelson didn't like to wash his face.
He didn't like to comb his hair.
He didn't like to take a bath.
He didn't like to clean his shoes.

If his fingernails were dirty . . . *"So what!"*
If his hands were grimy . . . *"Who cares?"*
If his shoelaces were dangling . . . *"Big deal!"*

Jason Nelson, Sammy's younger brother, was just the opposite. He really *liked* to keep himself neat and clean. After working in the garden, Jason took off his shoes and banged them together to shake out all the dirt. He scrubbed away the grime from his hands. He washed the soil and perspiration off his face. He ran a comb through his hair. It made him feel *good* to be clean and neat!

Their mother, Mrs. Nelson, often sent her two boys to Tucker's Grocery Store to get bread or milk. Sometimes she sent Sammy. And sometimes she sent Jason.

When Sammy entered the grocery store, Mr. Tucker, would say,

"Good morning, Sammy! How are you today?" Sammy would hang his head and mutter, "Okay, I guess." Sammy knew he didn't look good, so he didn't feel good about himself. And because he didn't feel good about himself, he didn't act good either.

When Jason went to the store, Mr. Tucker would say, "Good morning, Jason! How are you today?" Jason would look him straight in the eye and answer him with a big smile. "I'm *great*, Mr. Tucker!" Jason felt good about himself. And because he felt good about himself, he acted good also.

One day the telephone rang at Sammy and Jason's home. Their mother answered the phone. It was Mr. Tucker, the grocery man. He said, "Mrs. Nelson, I need a boy to work for me in my grocery store this summer. I will pay him well."

Mrs. Tucker replied, "I'm sure that either of my two boys would be happy to have a summer job. Sammy is the older one. Should I send him to see you?"

"No," Mr. Tucker replied. "Please ask Jason to come see me."

Jason went to see Mr. Tucker. Mr. Tucker hired him, and Jason started working in Tucker's Grocery Store. Each week he saved the money he earned to buy a new bike. He already had a new one picked out—the shiny red bike in the window of Johnson's Bike Store down the street.

Sammy felt bad that he didn't have a summer job like his younger brother. And he needed to earn money for a new bike, too. He had his eye on the shiny blue bike in the window of Johnson's Bike Store. But he had no money, and he had no job. Each time he talked to a boss, the answer was always, "Sorry, we can't use you."

Sammy wondered, *Why doesn't anyone want me to hire me? Why didn't Mr. Tucker want to hire me?*

One day when Sammy was in the grocery store buying bread for his mother, an idea came to him. *Maybe if I ask Mr. Tucker, he'll tell me why he chose Jason instead of me!* When no one was in the store, he asked him.

Mr. Tucker was quiet for a moment. He didn't know what to say. Then he decided to simply tell Sammy the truth. He knew that would be the kindest thing he could do for him.

"Sammy," Mr. Tucker commenced gently, "I'm sure you are a good boy, but it's easy to see that you don't take care of yourself. And if you don't take good care of your *own self*, it's doubtful that you would take good care of things on the job either. And no boss ever wants to hire a careless worker."

Sammy was silent for a moment. He was surprised at Mr. Tucker's words. Sure! He knew he was careless about cleanliness and neatness . . . but he thought it didn't matter.

Mr. Tucker patted him on the shoulder. "You are young, Sammy," he said. "You can change. You can start changing *today!* And mark my words—it *will* make a difference. You'll be able to find a job."

Sammy thanked Mr. Tucker. He walked slowly home, thinking hard. Finally he made his decision. Yes, he *would* change. And he would start *right now!*

From that day forward . . .

Sammy *combed* his tousled hair!

He *washed* his grimy face!

He *scrubbed* his neck and ears!

He *cleaned* his dirty hands and fingernails.

Instead of throwing his clothes on the floor, he hung them up so they wouldn't get all rumpled!

Did Mr. Tucker's words come true? Yes, they did! Sammy started looking for a job and this time he *succeeded!* Sammy worked hard and saved his money. By the end of the summer, *two* new bikes rested side by side in the Nelson garage.

One was a shiny red, and the other, a shiny blue!

———————

"Cleanliness is indeed next to godliness"—John Wesley.

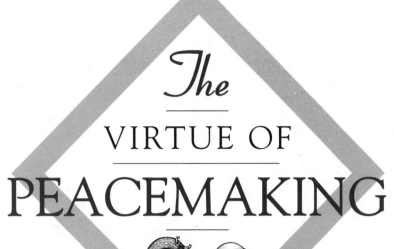

The
VIRTUE OF
PEACEMAKING

PEACEMAKERS
are always willing
to say
"I'm sorry,"
always willing to say,
"I forgive you!"
Always willing
to give up
their own rights
to make
peace.

SAY YOU ARE SORRY!

Quick, quick!
The sun goeth down!
Away with your anger!
Off with your frown!

Say you are sorry
Before you part,
So you'll go to bed
With a merry heart!

WE NEVER QUARREL

We never quarrel,
    We never fight!
That's why we're happy,
    Smiling and bright!

Why don't we quarrel?
    Why don't we fight?
The Bible says that
    It is not right!

◆ ◆ ◆

WHY SUZY FORGAVE BILLY

Suzy, Suzy!
    Weepy Suzy!
        Why do you sit and cry?
Billy, Billy,
    Willy-nilly!
        Poked his finger in my eye!
Suzy, Suzy!
    Smiling Suzy!
        What made your crying end?
Billy, Billy
    Said, "I'm sorry!
        Please be my friend again!"

HOW ABRAM SETTLED THE QUARREL

(Genesis 13:1-18)

Day after day they quarreled
And fought—
Those selfish servants
Of Abram and Lot.
"This land is ours!"
"Oh, no it's *not!*"
The servants shouted.
Their tempers were hot.
Then Abram said,
"Oh, please don't fight!
You choose the land
That's good in your sight.

If you choose the left,
Then I will go right.
Let's love one another
And be polite!"
So Lot chose the best,
And gave Abram the rest.
But for his kindness,
Abram was blessed.
God gave him riches
And silver and gold,
And years full of blessings
As Abram grew old.

"OL' MEANY McCRANK"

Once upon a time in a small village there lived an old man named Mr. McCrank. Everyone called him "Ol' Meany McCrank" because he was so hateful and mean. The family who lived next door to him became so distressed with his grumbling and fighting that they finally sold their home and moved away.

The Lovett family, who bought their house, did not know they were moving next door to such a mean neighbor. As soon as they started moving in, however, they began to hear about "Ol' Meany McCrank." The nearby neighbors said, "We hope he won't make you as miserable as the people who moved away!" This worried the Lovetts, but after talking it over, they vowed that they would show love to Mr. McCrank no matter how he might treat them.

The first thing Mrs. Lovett did to show friendliness was to take

Mr. McCrank a plate of freshly baked walnut cookies. Mr. McCrank took one look at the cookies and shoved the plate back into Mrs. Lovett's face. "Humph! *Walnut* cookies! I can't chew *walnuts!*" he said. Undaunted, she went home and baked some plain sugar cookies for him. He received them without a word. But as Mrs. Lovett walked back to her house, he watched her silently from his window.

The next morning Mr. Lovett took a stroll to look over their yard. As he stood admiring a large apple tree growing by their fence, he heard someone digging on the other side. It was Mr. McCrank working in his flower bed.

Mr. Lovett called out, "Good morning, Mr. McCrank!" Mr. McCrank glared at him over the fence. "Humph!" he grunted. "It's not a *good* morning at all! Look at my flower bed! If it weren't for your apple tree casting shade on my flowers, I might have some blooms!" He continued his weeding with a scowl on his face.

That afternoon one of the Lovett boys was batting balls in their yard. Suddenly his ball went

astray, flying high toward Mr. McCrank's house. *Crash!* It busted through his kitchen window! Mr. McCrank came running out of his house in a rage! He grabbed the Lovett boy and shook him wildly. When Mr. Lovett heard his son crying, he rushed outside. "What's wrong?" he asked. Mr. McCrank pointed to the broken window.

"Oh, Mr. McCrank, we're terribly sorry!" he said. " We'll replace the glass as soon as possible!" The next day they replaced the glass. But the new glass shined so brightly that it made all the other window glass look dull. So the Lovetts brought over a bucket of sudsy water and washed all the other windows. Mr. McCrank stood by the door, silently watching as his new neighbors washed all of his windows.

That night a blustery wind blew. When morning came, Mr. McCrank knocked furiously on the Lovetts' door. "Look at my yard!" he shouted. "The leaves from your maple tree have blown all over my lawn! If you don't rake them up right away, I'll bring over my garbage and dump it all over your lawn!"

The Lovett children hurried to get their jackets. They started raking leaves as fast as they could. When the yard was bare of leaves, Father Lovett noticed that the grass needed mowing. He brought over his lawn mower and mowed the entire lawn. Mr. McCrank watched silently from his window as his new neighbor mowed his lawn.

One day Mrs. Lovett noticed the village doctor entering Mr.

McCrank's house. As the doctor was leaving, she approached him. "Tell me, doctor. Is there anything we can do to help Mr. McCrank? Could we take him some food?"

"Of course," the doctor replied. "But he must eat only broth and gelatin for the next five days." So for the next five days one of the Lovetts took Mr. McCrank a kettle of steaming broth and a bowl of gelatin. Mr. McCrank accepted the food without a word. But each day as they left his house, he eyed them curiously from his bedroom window. This Lovett family puzzled him greatly.

By Sunday, Mr. McCrank was feeling fine. He sat by his window and watched the Lovetts as they walked happily toward their little corner church. All that day Mr. McCrank thought about the Lovett family. *Why do they treat me so nice? Why do they never become angry with me—no matter what I do?*

Finally Mr. McCrank decided that he had to find out if they were truly what they seemed to be. *Surely something will make them lose their patience with me! I'll give them a final test! I'll find out once and for all just how "loving" they really are!* He gazed toward the fence where the Lovetts' big apple tree was casting shade on his flower garden. "That's it!" he thought. "I'll chop down their apple tree!"

That night Mr. McCrank crept out of his house with a hatchet in his hand. He chopped . . . chopped . . . chopped! Finally the Lovetts' beautiful apple tree toppled to the ground!

When the Lovetts looked out the window the next morning, they were horrified to discover that their apple tree was lying on

the ground, its boughs still loaded with red apples. The children sobbed. Father Lovett looked very serious.

"It was wrong of Mr. McCrank to chop down our tree," he told his family. "He had no right to destroy what belonged to us. But we have vowed to always show him a loving, forgiving spirit. So let's do that right now." He thought for a moment, then spoke to the children.

"Go quickly, children!" he said. "Pick some apples off the boughs so Mother can bake Mr. McCrank an apple pie! Then get a big basket and fill it with the nicest apples you can find! Take the basket to Mr. McCrank along with

Mother's apple pie. *And be sure, children, to greet him with a loving smile!*"

Several hours later when Mr. McCrank opened his door, he could not believe his eyes! The Lovett children were standing there smiling up at him. One child handed him a warm apple pie. *It smelled delicious!* Another handed him a basket of shiny red apples. He stood there, stunned and speechless.

Several days passed by without any sign of Mr. McCrank. Then one morning the Lovetts heard a knock on their door. It was Mr. McCrank. He was standing there with his head hanging low. "Won't you come in?" they asked. Without a word he stepped inside. He took off his hat. He fumbled with it for a moment, twisting it in his hands.

Finally he spoke. "I'm sorry I cut down your apple tree!" he blurted out. "And I'm sorry for the way I've been treating you! You've been so kind to me that I'm ashamed of myself." He paused a moment. Then he stood straight and tall with his head held high. He looked them straight in the

eye. "I've decided I want to start being nice like you folks," he said, "and I'd like to go to church with you next week if you'll take me!"

From that day forward, Mr. McCrank was a new man. He accompanied the Lovetts regularly to the services at their little church on the corner. He started treating everyone in the village with kindness. He lived quietly and peacefully in his home until the day he died.

Before he died, he called Mr. Lovett to his side. "I've buried a bag of gold beneath my back porch," he said. "I want you to have it! You and your family have not only shown me love, but you've also shown me how to live. Because of you, I'm dying a better man—at peace with my fellow-man and with God!"

Mr. Lovett dug up the gold. When he asked his family what they should do with it, they thought of the church steeple which was almost ready to fall down and the cross at the top which was weather-beaten and cracked. So the Lovetts gave the money to the church. And in memory of Mr. McCrank, the church built a beautiful new steeple with a glistening golden cross on the top.

Every time the villagers walked by that street corner and saw the golden cross glistening atop the steeple, they thought lovingly of "Ol' Meany McCrank" who had become one of the kindest persons in their village.

The
VIRTUE OF
THE GOLDEN RULE

In any situation, ask yourself:
How would I want others
to treat me?
Whatever your answer,
that is what you should do.
Treat others as you
would want them
to treat you.

THE BEAR WHO DIDN'T CARE! (No, he really didn't!)

Benjamin Bear was happy, for he was going to the fair. Dressed in his new red jacket, he skipped down the road with his umbrella over his shoulder and his lunch bag swinging from his umbrella handle. Deep within the pocket of his new red jacket were five silver dollars that went "jingle . . . jangle . . . jingle" as he bounced along. Benjamin Bear was so happy that he burst out in song . . .

Oh, ho, ho! I'm a very happy bear!
I've got five dollars and I'm
going to the fair!

As Benjamin was singing, a small drop of rain landed on the tip of his nose. Then another . . . and another! Benjamin quickly opened his umbrella just before the rain poured down upon him. Snug and dry beneath his umbrella, Benjamin Bear went happily on his way dreaming about all the fun he was going to have at the fair.

Oh, ho, ho! I'm going to the fair!
I'll have a happy time when
I get there!

As Benjamin rounded the corner, he came upon an old man hobbling along with a cane. The rain was pouring down upon the old man's bare head. "Oh, Mr. Bear!" the old man cried. "I'm getting soaked! Would you be so kind as to let me walk along with you beneath your big umbrella?"

Benjamin thought, "This old man hobbles so slowly. I will never get to the fair if I share my umbrella with him." So Benjamin hurried along with his nose in the air singing . . .

I won't help you! I don't care!
I've got five dollars, and I'm
going to the fair!

Looking back, he saw the poor old man dripping wet in the rain as he hobbled down the road. And Benjamin Bear didn't care. No, he really didn't. Not a bit!

Soon the rain stopped and the sun came out again. Benjamin came to a steep hill. He huffed and he puffed as he climbed the hill. When he reached the top, he saw a plump, round-faced woman picking apples from a tree beside the road. When the woman heard footsteps approaching, she turned quickly and upset her basket. The apples went tumbling and bouncing down the road.

"Quick, Mr. Bear!" the woman shouted. "Help me! Grab the apples!"

Benjamin Bear looked down the steep hill. He was still breath-

ing hard from the climb. "I won't go down that hill again," he thought, "—not for anyone's apples!" So with his nose in the air, Benjamin hurried on singing . . .

I won't help you! I don't care!
I've got five dollars, and I'm
going to the fair!

Looking back, he saw the plump, round-faced woman scrambling after her apples as they rolled down the hill. And

Benjamin Bear didn't care. No, he really didn't. Not a bit!

Soon Benjamin came to a farmhouse. The farmer was drawing water from his well as fast as he could. His haystack was on fire,

and the wind was carrying the flames toward his barn.

"*Quick!* Mr. Bear, *Help me!* Grab a pail of water!" shouted the farmer. As the farmer ran with a pail of water, he splashed water all over his clothes. Benjamin Bear thought, "I don't want to splash water on my new red jacket. I want to look nice when I get to the fair!" So with his nose in the air, Benjamin hurried on singing . . .

> *I won't help you! I don't care!*
> *I've got five dollars and I'm*
> *going to the fair!*

Looking back, he saw the frantic farmer drawing another bucket of water as the wind blew flames toward his barn. And Benjamin Bear didn't care. No, he really didn't. *Not a bit!*

At last Benjamin arrived at the fair. Banners were waving, balloons were flying, bands were playing! Benjamin was excited. "I'm *glad* I arrived early!" he thought. "I'm *glad* I didn't let that hobbling old man slow me down in the rain!"

As Benjamin walked through the crowds, he puffed out his chest to make sure everyone saw his new red jacket. "I'm *glad* I can show off my new jacket!" he thought. "I'm *glad* I didn't spill water on it trying to put out the farmer's fire."

Soon Benjamin's legs began to feel a little tired. "I'm glad I still have strength to see more sights!" he thought. "I'm *glad* I didn't wear out my legs running after that old woman's apples."

But now Benjamin Bear was getting hungry. He decided it was time to eat his lunch. He found a quiet spot hidden away from the crowds in a grove of trees.

He hung his umbrella behind him on the limb of a tree. He took off his jacket and laid it carefully beside him so that he wouldn't spill food on it. He reached for his lunch bag. He started to draw out a

peanut butter sandwich, but stopped when he heard a noise behind him. Look-ing around, he saw a robber hiding behind the tree!

Before Benjamin could jump to his feet, the robber grabbed Ben-jamin's umbrella. He hit Benjamin Bear over the head with it! *BAM . . . BAM . . . BAM!!!* The um-brella broke into pieces.

As Benjamin lay on the ground, dazed and bruised, the robber ran away into the deep woods. Benjamin Bear was finally able to sit up. He looked for his new red jacket. It was gone—and along with his jacket, the five sil-ver dollars he kept in the pocket! He looked for his lunch. It was gone, too. He looked for his umbrella. It lay beside him on the ground, bent and broken.

What could he do now? His head hurt. He was weak and tired. He felt sick all over. There was nothing to do but go home.

So Benjamin Bear started walking home—trudging down the same road he had traveled a few hours before. But this time he was singing no happy song. He was carrying no umbrella over his shoulder with a lunch bag swinging from it. He was wearing no fine new jacket with silver dollars jingling in his pocket.

Benjamin Bear turned and looked back toward the fairgrounds. The banners were still waving . . . the balloons were still flying . . . the bands were still playing! Big fat teardrops welled up in Benjamin's eyes and rolled down his cheeks. Benjamin Bear felt very sad as he headed back home.

The road was dusty. The sun beat down upon Benjamin's aching head. His throat was dry. He was very thirsty. Soon

Benjamin came to the farmhouse where the farmer had been throwing water on his haystack fire. Benjamin thought, "Oh, how I'd like a drink of that fresh, cool water from the farmer's well!"

When Benjamin spotted the farmer working in his yard, he called to him. "Please, Mr. Farmer, may I have a drink of water to quench my thirst?" The farmer scowled at Benjamin Bear and answered him gruffly:

To quench my fire, you
helped me not!
To quench your thirst . . .
not one drop!

Benjamin could see it was hopeless. So down the road he walked, singing a sad song.

The farmer won't help me.
The farmer doesn't care!
Won't anyone take pity on a poor,
thirsty bear?

Soon Benjamin came to the steep hill where the plump, round-faced woman had spilled her apples. Benjamin thought, "Oh, how I'd like to eat one of those big, juicy apples!" He spotted the woman looking over the apples she had picked that day. Benjamin called to her. "Please, lady, may I have one of your apples to eat? I am weak from hunger!" The woman scowled at Benjamin Bear. She replied sternly:

You helped me not in
my time of need.
You'll get no apple—no, indeed!

Benjamin could see it was hopeless. So down the road he walked, singing a sad song:

The woman won't help me.
The woman doesn't care!
Won't anyone take pity on a poor,
hungry bear?

Soon the sun disappeared behind thick clouds. The sky grew dark. Thunder clapped overhead. Rain began to pour down on Benjamin's bare head. Not only was Benjamin hungry and thirsty, but now he was also getting drenched in the rain! He noticed a house at the end of a lane. As Benjamin drew closer, he could see a man on the porch, seated in a rocker. Yes, it was the old man whom he had met hobbling along in the rain that

morning. Benjamin Bear crept forward cautiously.

The old man rose and greeted him with a smile. "Hello, Mr. Bear!" he said. "What can I do for you?"

"Please, sir," Benjamin began, "I am dripping wet from the rain! Could I just stand under your porch roof until the storm blows over?" The old man graciously pointed to a bench on the porch. Smiling pleasantly, he said:

Do come and share my
porch with me!
We'll have a sandwich
and some tea!

A sandwich? Some tea? Those words sounded good to hungry, thirsty Benjamin. But Benjamin Bear was puzzled. *Why was the old man treating him so kindly? Had the old man forgotten that he had refused to share his umbrella with him that morning?*

The old man laid down a big black book he had been reading, and went into the house to fix sandwiches and tea. Benjamin Bear sat down on the bench beside the empty rocker where the man had left the big book. It was spread wide open. Benjamin's eyes lit on some words underlined in red:

> *Do unto others as you would have them do unto you.*

Benjamin Bear read the words again thoughtfully. He gulped hard. *Is this what the old man believes—that he should treat others the same way he would want to be treated himself? Is this why he was being so kind to him?* Benjamin decided it must be so. He sat quietly for a moment. Then he hung his head in shame.

How sorry he was that he had refused to share his umbrella with the old man! How sorry he was that he'd refused to help gather the woman's spilled apples! How sorry he was that he had refused to help the farmer put out his fire!

At that very moment, as he sat quietly on the old man's porch,

Benjamin Bear made himself a promise. Deep within his heart he promised that never again would he sing the words, *I won't help you! I don't care!* And with that promise, Benjamin Bear found a new song coming into his heart. From that day forward . . . forever after . . . whenever Benjamin Bear came upon anyone in need, he sang his new song:

> *Oh, ho, ho!*
> *I'm a happy helping bear!*
> *Why do I help you?*
> *Because I really care!*

And the best thing about it was this: Benjamin Bear *did* care! Yes, he *really did!*

A RULE TO REMEMBER

It was Jeff's first day at a new school. When he arrived home, his mother asked, "How was school?"

"It was *awful!*" Jeff replied. "No one talked to me, no one ate lunch with me, no one played with me!"

"Don't feel bad," his mother said. "You'll soon make new friends." Her words came true. In time Jeff made many new friends.

One day another new boy arrived at school. His name was Steve. Jeff could see he felt lonely. Jeff remembered how he felt on his first day at the new school. He also remembered a Bible truth his dad had taught him—the "Golden Rule."

"In any situation," his dad had said, "ask yourself this question: 'How would I want others to treat *me?*' Whatever your answer, son, that's how you should treat *others!*"

Jeff remembered exactly how he had wanted others to treat him on his first day at the new school. He had wanted his new classmates to be friendly. Jeff decided, "I will be friendly to Steve." So he ate lunch with him, played ball with him, and waved a friendly goodbye to him when school was over.

When Steve arrived home, his mother said, "How do you like your new school, Steve?"

"It was *great!*" he replied happily. "But at first I felt terribly lonely. Then a boy named Jeff made friends with me. *He seemed to know exactly how I was feeling!* It sure made a difference!"

That evening Jeff confided in his dad, "I'm glad you taught me the Golden Rule. I needed to remember that rule today."

Jeff's dad looked pleased. "It's a good rule to remember *every* day, son!"

Jeff nodded. He knew his dad was right!

The VIRTUE OF HONORING PARENTS

We HONOR
OUR PARENTS
by obeying them,
by showing them love,
by listening to them,
by respecting their authority.
God is pleased when we
honor our parents.
He has promised to bless us
for doing so.

HOW THE BEARS SHOWED THEIR LOVE

Father, what can I do for you
To show you love today?
I'll bring you frosty lemonade
With cookies on a tray!

Mother, what can I do for you
To show how dear you are?
I'll bring you yellow daffodils
And put them in a jar!

THE OBEDIENT BOY JESUS

"Jesus dear, Jesus dear!
It's time for you to rise!"

"I am coming, Mother!
I'm opening up my eyes!"

"Jesus boy, Jesus boy!
It's time for us to pray!"

"I will come, Father!
I'll come without delay!"

"Jesus dear, Jesus dear!
Bring me corn to grind!"

"I will bring it, Mother!
I will quickly mind!"

"Jesus boy, Jesus boy!
Help me clean this room!"

"Yes, I will, Father!
I'll sweep it with my broom!"

"Jesus dear, Jesus dear!
You are a special son!
Of all the children in the world—
Like you, there isn't one!"

A VALENTINE FOR MOTHER

I made a valentine today.
    I made it for my mother.
I drew a great big heart to say
    How dearly that I love her.

I colored it with color crayons
    And pasted lace around it.
I placed it by the mailbox,
    And waited till she found it.

I waited and I waited
    Till she came to get the mail.
At last I saw her coming,
    Slowly walking down the trail.

And when she found the valentine,
    She said, "What can this be?
Did someone really send this
    Pretty valentine to me?"

And when she paused beside the post,
    I jumped out from behind it!
I said, "Oh, Mommy dearest!
    I thought you'd never find it!"

She said, "I love my valentine!
    How nicely you have drawn it!
With roses red and violets blue,
    And lacy ruffles on it!"

And then she hugged me close to her,
    And said, "Dear child of mine,
How good of you to show me love
    With this sweet valentine!"

THE SON WHO DISHONORED HIS FATHER

(Luke 15:11-24)

There once was a son
    who left his home,
He asked for his money
    and started to roam.

He spent all he had,
    and soon he was sad.
And so he began
    to weep and to moan.

"Why," he cried,
    "did I go away?
And why must I feed
    these pigs all day?
I'm hungry for even
    a crust of bread.
The pigs in this pen
    are all better fed.
My father's house is
    full of good meat.
Even his servants have
    plenty to eat."

The son hurried home
    to his father that day,

And this is what
    he had to say:

"Forgive me, Father,
    for all I have done.
I'm no longer worthy
    to be called your son.

"I've come back home,
    and I want to stay.
So make me as one of your
    servants, I pray."

The father cried out,
    "My son is here!
Rejoice with me!
    Spread the good cheer!

"Bring him a robe!
    Give him some shoes!
Tell everybody!
    Spread the good news!

"Invite everyone from the
    great to the least

"To come and be merry
    and have a great feast!

"And put on his finger
    a fine golden ring.
My son has come home!
    Let everyone sing!"

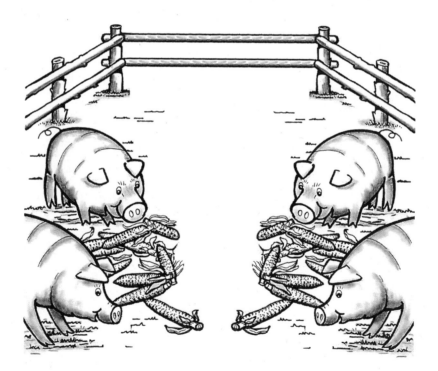

The
VIRTUE OF
HONORING GOD

*We HONOR GOD by
worshiping Him each week,
by obeying His Word,
by telling others
about His great love.
We honor God
by showing respect
for His name
and respect for
His house of worship.*

THIS BUNNY RABBIT

This bunny rabbit
went to Bible school

This sleepy bunny
stayed home.

This bunny rabbit
learned a Bible verse.

This lazy bunny
learned none.

This bunny rabbit
had a happy time.

This grumpy bunny
was bored.

This bunny rabbit
sang a happy tune,

Singing praises
to the Lord!

"Let us go into the house of the LORD"—Psalm 122:1.

I HAVE TEN DIMES!

With one I'll buy
    a whistle to blow.
With one I'll buy
    some seeds to grow.

With one I'll buy
    a gift for my mother.
With one I'll buy
    a toy for my brother.

With one I'll buy
    a book to read.
With one I'll buy
    a pencil I need.

With one I'll buy
    a fish for my tank.
And one I'll save
    in my piggy bank.

With one I'll buy
    a brand-new rule,
And one I'll take
    to Bible school . . .

To give to God
    who loves me so
And gives me
    good things
       here below.

I'M GOING TO BIBLE SCHOOL!

"Why are you waking so early, Ted?"
    "I'm going to Bible school!" he said.

"Why are you jumping right out of bed?"
    "I'm going to Bible school!" he said.

"Why are you brushing the hair on your head?"
    "I'm going to Bible school!" he said.

"Why are you mending your shirt with the thread?"
    "I'm going to Bible school!" he said.

"Why are you eating your berries and bread?"
    "I'm going to Bible school!" he said.

"Who will go with you, little Ted?"
    "Betty and Bobby and Sue and Ned!

"Daddy will pull the little red sled,
    And we'll all go to Bible school!" he said.

I SHALL BLESS THE LORD!

Bless Him, Betty! Bless Him, Ben!
Jesus is your finest Friend!

Bless Him, Patty! Bless Him, Paul!
Jesus loves you one and all!

Bless Him, Sammy! Bless Him, Sue!
Jesus Christ has died for you!

Debbie . . . . . Cindy . . . . . Bill . . . . . and Jeff!
Bless the Lord who gives you breath!

Cathy . . . . Mary . . . . . . John . . . and Ted! Bless the Lord for daily bread!

Julie . . . . Bob . . . . and (_____), too!
your name
Bless the Lord who cares for you!

ANNIE AND HER BIBLE

Little Annie Crocker sat upon her rocker,
    Reading her Bible on her knee.
Along came her teacher with the village preacher,
    And said, "What a blessed child is she!"

"From a child thou hast known the holy scriptures"—2 Timothy 3:15.

My Prayer

*Lord, I want to please You, for You are the One
who has given me breath and life.*

*Day by day I want to do the things that will help
me become a better child.*

*Even though I am still young, I know my
character is being formed within me each day
by every choice I make—*

*whether to do right or to do wrong . . .
whether to be generous or to be selfish . . .
whether to tell the truth or to deceive . . .
whether to be loving or to be hateful . . .
whether to be ambitious or to be lazy . . .
whether to obey or to disobey . . .*

*Lord, please help me to make good choices, so
that I will be a child who pleases You and is blessed
with a happy life, making others happy, too.*

Amen.

My Pledge

Each day as God helps me, I will do my best . . .

- ◆ *To be honest and truthful,*

- ◆ *To be loyal, cheerful, and courteous,*

- ◆ *To be generous, friendly, and kind to others,*

- ◆ *To be thankful for all things God gives me,*

- ◆ *To honor my body by keeping it clean and neatly clothed,*

- ◆ *To learn how to work with my hands,*

- ◆ *To always be quick to say "I'm sorry,"*

- ◆ *To treat others in the same way that I would want them to treat me,*

- ◆ *To show loyalty and respect to my parents and family,*

- ◆ *To honor and obey my parents and God.*